Pieces Of Me

Marissa Van Dalen

BookLeaf
Publishing

Presentation by *BookLeaf Publishing*

Web: www.bookleafpub.com

E-mail: info@bookleafpub.com

ISBN: 978-93-95890-53-3

First edition 2022

DEDICATION

To You:

You did this. All on your own. You are strong. You are amazing. You got this.

ACKNOWLEDGEMENT

To my children, Jayden, Arya and Lyanna: thank you for being the light in my life and giving me courage to do things I would have never considered before. This, as is everything I do, is for you.

To my mum, Jenny: thank you for instilling in me a passion for words and writing and reading and all the things I love, you are amazing. You've always believed in me and encouraged me to follow my heart and I can never thank you enough.

To my girlfriends: Naomi, Sherry, Leah, Di, Liza, Casey, Centaine, Jess, Tina, Bec, Ange, you guys have had my back through so much stuff. You are amazing, all of you, and I love you so much. Thank you all for believing in me and giving me courage to try new things. No girl has a better group of friends. You are top tier women, and you help this queen straighten her crown.

To M: Thank you for the inspiration. Don't know how you'll feel about this, don't really care either!

PREFACE

I was inspired to write the poems contained in this book by a few things: the breakdown of my marriage, which completely blindsided me; the loss of my son in 2016, who was stillborn; my amazing group of girl friends who have held me up through these hard times like absolute champions; my kids, who light my way through the dark times and other losses and hard times that make us question everything.

The real challenge when writing about things of this nature is looking inward and having the courage to write about your feelings, especially for someone like me, who is uncomfortable with that kind of thing. Which is another reason I decided to participate; I need to get more comfortable with opening up.

This book came about because I entered a 21 Day Poetry Challenge, and I thought, why the heck not? I've written new works, and have included some of my older stuff that I had written down in an old notebook that nobody else has ever read. I decided to be brave and put myself out there.

Anyway, I hope you enjoy it, because I enjoyed writing it.

Alone

The darkness surrounds me
Comforting in its dark embrace
I feel at peace here
Though I am alone

On my own with my thoughts
Tears sting my eyes
My thoughts inevitably turn to you
And the bitterest of goodbyes

You took everything I gave you
Tore it up, threw it away
Like they mean nothing at all
But I will not beg you to stay.

You broke me down
Until there was nothing left
You stole my comfort
Left me bereft.

Surrounded by this darkness
I am comforted, I am home
I don't need you anymore
I am just fine here alone.

To Me

You are worthy
You are wild
You are passionate
You are amazing
You are wonderful
You are fierce
You are a fighter
You are strong
You will endure

Follow your heart
Dream big
Love hard
Because, my darling,
You are everything.

You are enough.

Apology

I owe myself an apology
For putting up with too much
Too much I did not deserve.

I owe myself an apology
For settling for you

I owe myself an apology
For thinking this is what I deserve

I owe myself an apology
For caving in to you

I owe myself an apology
For putting my faith in you.

I Deserve

I deserve respect
I deserve love
I deserve happiness
I deserve to have my faith rewarded
I deserve to get back the good I put out
I deserve someone brave
I deserve loyalty
I deserve kindness
I deserve understanding
I deserve someone who thinks I am amazing
I deserve safety
I deserve great things
I deserve better than I got from you.

Arya

My sunshine girl
my ray of light
the light that called to me
when I struggled in the night.

Your pure heart is beautiful,
your attitude scary
They say you always get one like you-
I definitely did, and it's you.

So headstrong and full of will
Your heart is full of love
My wish is that you'll stay this way,
That no one dulls your shine.

I love you, sweet girl.
Forever and always.

Please Remember Me

I stand upon the shore behind you
The wind whips your hair around your face
The tears flow freely down your cheeks.
I reach out to touch you, but you recoil
I remember the day I left you,
Calling out my name.
You thought you lost me that day,
But truthfully you lost me before
The rush of pain and loneliness
Is not something you can ignore.
Vilify me if you will,
Call me every name under the sun,
Be angry with me
Be afraid of what's to come
Call me still the one.
I love you so much I can barely breathe
I didn't want to leave you,
I didn't want to cause you pain
I still want you to believe in me.
Remember the times we used to have,
The good ones and the bad
Remember the times when I made you laugh,
And the ones that made you sad.
Remember my smile, my heart, my face,
The way I held you in my arms.

Remember the way I loved you,
Remember everything about me,
For I am always near.

Lonely

This empty feeling
Growing deep inside me
I don't want you to see
You know it too well...
Know me too well.

It eats at me, gnawing, clawing,
Devouring
Until I'm all undone.
I sit and stare
Feeling lonely and alone
Seeing all these people
Who love and are loved in return.

Still this feeling eats my insides,
I feel so empty,
like there's nothing there.
I'm waiting, waiting, waiting
Waiting to be complete.

I sit in the rain.
Alone again
The empty feeling grows stronger,
It's taken over my heart.
I wonder how much longer I'll have to wait

Until it's my turn.

I'm alone.
No one to love me, no one to care
I'm nothing but empty darkness,
Sitting all alone.

I Miss You

I stumble in the doorway
I hear you're gone
Out of my life
Gone forever long.

The words scream
Through my head
Bouncing, echoing...
Saying that you're dead.

You left me
At the worst time of my life
The words that told your fate
cut through me like a knife.

I'm so hurt, so angry.
Why, Daddy, why?
Why did you leave me here?
Why did you make me cry?

Your leaving hurt me so,
I push my love aside
The joy has left my life
The day I heard you died.

I try to compreheand
The reason, the rhyme.

I've pushed everyone aside
I hide the real me
When they look into my eyes
I wonder what they see.

Do they see anger?
Do they see pain?

The sun will never shine the same
The flowers won't bloom as well,
but no matter how much it hurts,
I remember how much I love you.

Daddy, I miss you.

Reflection

It's funny how
a lie discovered
is the perfect way
to move on from heartbreak.

I wasn't sure I could lose you
nor live without you
but the discovery of the depths of your betrayals
knocked that feeling right out of me.

It's more and more every week,
something new you've done
a new lie uncovered.

I wish you had courage:
Courage to love me
courage to leave me
Instead you were a coward.

And now you don't have me at all.

The End

Nothing in this world
prepared me for you
Neither your coming;
nor for your leaving.

You were the light in my darkness
a balm for my damaged soul
I truly thought you were the one
But you weren't, were you? At all.

Losing you was hard enough
without all the other lies.
Tell me, did I deserve this?
Because all I did was love you.

I tore myself apart to give you what you wanted
lost who I was along the way
Instead of helping me find me again
you looked the other way

All of this has left me broken
but I am fighting my way back
Despite you, and all your lies
I am determined to win.

I will always love you
that will never change
but I love the memory of the old you
Not the person you became.

Coward

I loved you
Gave you everything I had in me
I trusted you
You took that trust and smashed it
Begged me for a family
I gave it
I asked you to devote yourself to me,
You would never.
I I look at you and all I see now
Is a weak man.
Selfish, unkind.
You had everyone fooled, didn't you.
Such a good guy, they said.
If only they knew
You are NOT brave
You are NOT strong.
I am too much for you, too difficult
You were too weak to tame me.
You are a coward.

Bruised, not Broken

I'm bruised, not broken
You paused me, not stopped me
I am too much for you...
Too intense, feel too much
Too stubborn, too wild.

You hurt me, not broke me
You stole a piece of my soul
I will never get it back.

I take each day
Step by step, inch by inch
I am finding my way forward
Figuring out what I want
Who I am.

I am strong, a fighter
I'd have fought for you if you were worth it
I am kind, and soft
A phoenix rising from the ashes of your lies.

I am bruised, not broken.

Sorry

Sorry I'm unrelenting
Unforgiving
Sorry I'm hurting you
That I've been hurt
Sorry I won't change my opinions
Sorry for being me.

Sorry for caring about your heart
Wanting to keep you safe
Sorry for being the person I am
Sorry for saving your life.

Sorry that I bore you,
Sorry that I'm strong
Sorry for having weak moments,
Wasn't aware that that was wrong.

Sorry I'm not the one you want to love you
I have a lot of faults
Sorry for being the anchor
That was weighing you down

Sorry I tried to save you
From heartache and pain
Once your heart is broken

You will never be the same.

I'm setting you free now
Make your own mistakes
Sorry if this makes you mad,
I'm sure I will forever.

I Wish

I wished for you
On a starry night
Not knowing who you are,
But you feel so right

You're unknown to me,
A perfect stranger
I wished for you though,
So my heart would know no danger

I wished for a man
Who could love me for me
Never ask something of me I could not give
Who makes me feel complete.

You'd take the best of me with the bad
My weakness with my strength
My bravery with my fear
And hold me when I'm wrong.

You'd always be there
through thick and thin
You'd be there when I lose the battle,
You'd be there when I win.

I made a wish for you
Upon the evening star
I know you don't exist though,
It's fun to wonder where you are.

True Love

You're always there for me,
no judgement, just love
You hold me above water,
keep me from drowning.
You rally round me
when I need you.
You give me strength
when I keep none for myself.
Your friendship means the world to me
you shower me in love
You always tell me the truth,
no matter how hard to hear-
because we both value it.
When times are tough, you help me stand tall
give me strength to get through it all.
My friends are my true loves-
Yes, sometimes we argue and disagree,
but at the end of the day,
it's all love.
Thank you, all of you-
Thank you for the kindness,
the love, the honesty, the loyalty,
lending me your strength.
I am lucky to have you, all of you.

Thank you for being the best damn friends a girl
can have.
You are my truest and dearest loves.

I love you all. Forever.

Buttons

You push my buttons
You know how to get me
You know how to break me
How to shake me.

You know my fears, my pet hates
Know what angers me
And you use it to your advantage
When you want to get your way.

You know my jealousies
And insecurities
You manipulate those feelings
To get inside my head, make me feel unworthy.

You push those buttons to make me mad...
But all you do is make me sad.

Jayden

My boy, my heart
my brave protector,
my truest love.
You always speak your mind
Always tell me true
You love me as fiercely
as I love you.
You are so smart and funny,
an excellent big brother and oh so kind.
You are one who values honesty,
a trait that's hard to find.
Stay fierce, my boy.
Stay kind.
Your mama will always love you
Until the end of time.

Fighter

I won't let you drag me down
I won't let you wound me
I won't let you hurt me
I won't let you scare me.
I am a fighter
I will fight until I die
I will go down kicking and screaming,
Raising unholy hell.
I am strong and I am brave
I don't know how to lose
You can hit me all you want,
I won't let you win.
I will survive
I will prosper.
If I cry, you will never see it
I am NOT afraid.
You can't hurt me.
I am proud and fierce and glorious...
I am a fighter.
And you will never beat me.

Lyanna

An unexpected blessing
I loved you from the moment I knew
The child I was always meant to have,
the child of my soul.
You, my darling, are full of fire
Of laughter and joy
Oh, you can get grumpy
but even then, you're still my sweetheart.
You're always on the go,
always looking for something to do.
You make me melt when you give me kisses
and say 'Mama, love you'.

I love you, my fierce, wild child.
More than anything on this earth.

Being Mama

I created you
I loved you the moment I knew
You borrowed the best of me to make you.
You changed my life
Turned it upside down
But I would not change a thing.
You make me whole
Complete me
You vex me and test me
You bring me joy
You make me happy
You are my truest loves
You are the things I never knew I needed.
I never saw myself as a mother
It was never my dream
But you came along
And changed everything.
You broke my heart wide open
Gave me love I never understood
I knew I'd die for you,
And lord I still would.
You all drive me crazy
But life is never dull
I would change nothing about any of you...
Except maybe the volume.

You are all perfect to me
You are my dearest ones,
My greatest loves.
My pride, my joy, my heart.
I am not a perfect person,
But I did three things perfectly-
You.

I love you more than anything
More than words can adequately express...
I hope one day you read this,
And know that Mama loves you best.

Broken Dreams

Every parents worst nightmare
is losing a child.
You have your hopes
your dreams...
What will they look like?
Who will they be like?
How they'll smile. Laugh.
You have images in your mind
You're excited.
You chatter endlessly about them...
Everyone gets tired of hearing it...
You don't care, because you're happy....

And then... it's gone.
Poof! Just like that.
Hopes shattered, dreams dead, hearts broken.
It feels like you'll never smile again.
Like you'll never stop crying.
Life goes on around you,
and inside, you are dying.
Your heart is broken,
Your head is foggy,
Your arms, empty.
It's like you're drowning and no one can save
you.

It's a hole that nothing can ever fill,
nothing makes any of it any better.
The people who love you surround you,
shower you with love...
But they don't understand...
And you always feel alone.

I dream of you most nights,
You're always in my thoughts.
I am not the person I used to be...
How could I be?
To lose someone I love so much?
I'm still me but...
My smile is not quite as joyful...
my eyes seem a little sadder...
I hold my loved ones tighter.
Losing you changed my life,
but loving you did too.

I still have hopes and dreams for you,
it's silly, but that's just me.
I know you're always with me,
hanging out by my side...
I wish things were different:
That you were here.
That I could hold you
Listen to you laugh
and fight with your siblings,
teach you how to bake.

So many things to show you...
But they just happen in my dreams...
Because you're not here.
And I can't hold you.
The pieces of my heart will never mend.
I carry you with me, everywhere I go...
But you carry a piece of me too.